Minute Motivators for Women

Stan & Linda Toler

BEACON HILL PRESS
OF KANSAS CITY

Copyright © 2010, 2014 by Stan Toler and Linda Toler

Beacon Hill Press of Kansas City
PO Box 419527
Kansas City, MO 64141
BeaconHillBooks.com

ISBN 978-0-8341-3288-7

Printed in the
United States of America

Library of Congress Control Number: 2014934927

10 9 8 7 6 5 4 3 2 1

Introduction

If it's true that behind every good man is a great woman, then you've got an important job! Women are influencers. You influence your husbands, your children, your church community, your coworkers, your neighbors. That means you have a big responsibility. Scripture says, "From everyone who has been given much, much will be demanded; and from the one who has been entrusted with much, much more will be asked" (Luke 12:48).

Understanding how important you are will hopefully inspire you to constantly improve yourself. As flight attendants say on every trip, "In an emergency, put your own mask on before assisting others." In other words, take care of yourself so you won't be a burden to others; once you're squared away, you'll be a great help to everyone around you!

Take some time right now to put that mask on. One minute could make all the difference for you and for those around you.

—Stan & Linda Toler

Be yourself.

To be yourself in a world that is
constantly trying to make you
something else is the greatest
accomplishment.

—Ralph Waldo Emerson

AUTHENTICITY

Everyone knows that faking righteousness doesn't work. Even Jesus accepted sinners while condemning hypocrites. But don't confuse authenticity with laziness. Be yourself—don't be one person at church and an entirely different person at work or home—but be careful to recognize that what feels easiest isn't always the most authentic.

Being real doesn't give you the freedom to express all the negative thoughts in your head ("I'm just saying it like it is"); being real doesn't mean you ought to give in to destructive personality traits ("That's just who I am"). That's not who you are! The real you is fighting against your inner self, and by resisting the urge to speak unkindly or to be manipulative or to feed an addiction or to lose your temper, the real you becomes stronger.

To be who you really are, you have to know yourself. You are a child of God, made in His image, the crown of His creation. You are beautiful, strong, creative, intelligent, kind, and precious. Be that person. Be who you really are. Even when it's tough!

God designed you to be a woman of character. Fight hard against every internal and external force that tempts you to forget who you really are. Confess your sins and shortcomings, and embrace your God-given personality and skills. Then you will truly be authentic.

Capitalize on your strengths.

A woman of mystique is fully aware of her flaws and weaknesses, yet she is strong enough to admit them and not be embarrassed by them.

—Jean Lush

STRENGTH

They say most people need ten compliments for every one criticism. Usually this is an admonition to encourage each other, which we should do; but doesn't such a fact beg the question? Why do people need so much praise? Why are we letting our mistakes matter to us more than our accomplishments?

It seems counterintuitive to say that focusing on our strengths is more humble than focusing on our weaknesses; but perhaps pride is exactly what keeps us chewing on criticisms. A humble person is comfortable with not being highly esteemed and so is not distracted by her weaknesses. On the other hand, a person desperate to make others believe she can handle any situation that comes her way with skill and finesse—who attempts to defy the statement that nobody is perfect—has an ego problem.

It's certainly okay to try to improve ourselves; the problem comes when we spend all our energy correcting our weaknesses rather than utilizing our strengths. We would be much more effective in every endeavor, including our work for the Lord, if we compensated for our weaknesses through teamwork—using our God-given talents to bless others, and letting them use theirs to bless us.

Ask for advice.

Fools think their own way is right,

but the wise listen to others.

—Proverbs 12:15

WISDOM

Seeking out advice is unpopular; asking what others think is perceived as a lack of self-confidence or even personal weakness. "You've got to do what works for you," is a likely answer you'll receive if you ask for input about a personal decision. Ask for help in a business situation, and people may question if you know how to do your job.

In a culture where truth is perceived as relative and morality silly, we convince ourselves that we know best—and we surround ourselves with people who will support our decisions rather than make us think them through.

Wisdom, however, is cultivated through thoughtful, prayerful contemplation in the context of community. Experience really does provide insight, so respecting our elders makes sense. People removed from the situation really might be able to see more clearly, so listening to them works. Good decisions really do matter, so seeking wisdom is worth the effort.

Enjoy waiting.

Patience is waiting. Not passively waiting. That is laziness. But to keep going when the going is hard and slow—that is patience.

—Source Unknown

PATIENCE

If you've ever had to wait for something important—like test results from a doctor's office, or a baby to be born or adopted, or a job offer, or a marriage proposal—you understand what it means to be out of control. You've done everything you can, and there is nothing more you can do. You cannot control what happens next; you can't even control how long you have to wait for your answer.

Living with the unknown understandably evokes anxiety in people. The good news is that it doesn't have to. It is possible to experience this time of waiting with great peace—the kind of peace that passes understanding. By knowing God's character and experiencing His love, you learn to trust Him. He knows better than you do what is best for you—and He has the power to make it happen. His plans and His timing are flawless.

Letting go of your anxiety and resting in Him feels kind of like turning the wheel over to another person when you're too sleepy to drive. It's a relief. You can sit back and enjoy the journey, or take a nap, or care for children in the back seat. Likewise, when you give your burden to God, you can enjoy your day-to-day moments, rest, or reach out to others.

Send Thank You notes.

Some people grumble because roses have thorns; I am thankful that the thorns have roses.

—Alphonse Karr

GRATEFULNESS

This is not an etiquette book. I don't know how soon you need to send Thank You notes after a shower or whether you need to send one to your boss for the bonus you received; what I know is what Scripture says: "Out of the overflow of his heart his mouth speaks" (Luke 6:45). In other words, your attitude will affect your behavior. If you cultivate an attitude of gratefulness, Thank You notes will follow. If you recognize the good thing another person has done for you, you'll want to let them know it.

The key, then, is to feel grateful. How do we do that? Do we compare ourselves to those in third-world countries? Maybe not. That often creates guilt or even arrogance instead of thanksgiving. And let's be real. When life is stressful, and people are annoying (or mean!), and we just can't seem to get ahead, it's just not realistic to thank our lucky stars that we don't have malaria. (Besides, it's very possible for people in the worst possible situations to be thankful too.)

Thankfulness comes when we are able to step back from whatever circumstances we are in and see ourselves as a part of the whole. When we know our purpose goes beyond our personal happiness, every act of kindness can be recognized as bonus, and we are thankful.

Stick with your plan.

Once you have made up your
mind, stick to it; there is no
longer any 'if' or 'but'.

—Napoleon Bonaparte

PERSISTENCE

We all have goals for ourselves—whether it's to diet or exercise or read the Bible regularly or volunteer or take a course or call a friend. But then that bowl of ice cream calls our name; hitting the treadmill sounds miserable; making time for devotions or volunteering seems impossible; pursuing our goals and our friends just never happens.

Why don't we do the things we want to do?

Because we think about it.

We can make good decisions in the quiet of the day—to start getting up earlier in the mornings, to go back to church, to quit drinking. But if we rethink those good decisions when the alarm clock goes off, when the Sunday newspaper is especially interesting, when our friends invite us out, then we will almost definitely take the easier path. The trick is to not rethink our good decisions, especially when the moment is upon us. If something is on the list of things to do, do it. It's as simple as that.

Simple doesn't mean easy, of course. Our minds will begin to come up with brilliant excuses to ignore our own mandate—so we have to intentionally push those thoughts away and get moving.

Do something you're scared to do.

Get used to being uncomfortable.
It is uncomfortable doing something
that's risky. But so what?
Do you want to stagnate and
just be comfortable?

—Barbra Streisand

RISK-TAKING

Risk-taking just for the thrill of it is not wise; but avoiding risk just for the safety of it is no wiser. Either way it's an emotional rather than rational—or faith-based—decision.

The longing for security is a strong emotion that can easily paralyze us without our even realizing it. We choose careers we hate because it's more stable than our dream job or the missions field where we feel called. We stay in abusive relationships because it's better than no relationship. We don't grow in our faith because God might turn our whole world upside down.

Many of us would rather stay in a bad place than to venture into the unknown. It's time to break away from that kind of destructive thinking! It's time to take one obedient step forward. It's time to trust God!

You may not be ready for that one big leap of faith that you know is before you, so start with something smaller. Do something you know God wants you to do that scares you just a bit. Say hello to the homeless man you pass every day on your way to work; introduce yourself to a newcomer at church; pray out loud. As you obey God in the little things, you'll see how good He is, and you'll be encouraged to obey Him in something big.

Learn a new skill.

All of the top achievers I know
are life-long learners . . . looking
for new skills, insights, and
ideas. If they're not learning,
they're not growing . . . not moving
toward excellence.

—Denis Waitley

LEARNING

One law of nature seems to be that it is impossible to be still; if we're not moving forward, we're moving backwards. Just look at any garden: If the gardener is regularly tending it, it flourishes; if the garden is neglected for even a short time, it becomes an ugly mess. Take marriage: If both spouses are giving each other love and respect, all is well; if either one neglects those basic requirements the relationship blows up. Exercising works the same way: Steady consistent workouts create a fit body; neglecting exercise causes the body to quickly decline.

To keep yourself moving forward, challenge yourself to learn a new skill. Take piano lessons. Audit a course at your local university. Learn a new sport, like racquetball or swimming or rollerblading or golf. Give your devotional time a boost by delving into theology, so you'll have clear sense of what you believe and why.

Don't fool yourself into thinking it's okay to take a break from growing. We must be actively pursuing ways to improve ourselves spiritually, intellectually, emotionally, relationally, and physically.

Join a prayer group.

Therefore confess your sins to

each other and pray for each other

so that you may be healed.

The prayer of a righteous man

is powerful and effective.

—James 5:16

PRAYER

People attend prayer meetings for various reasons: for personal support, to cry out to God on behalf of a person in crisis or a world event, to cover the church in prayer, to seek wisdom and guidance. The ultimate purpose, of course, is to connect with God.

Various things result from prayer meetings: comfort, direct answers to prayer, unity and effectiveness in ministry, insight for living. The ultimate result, of course, is connection with God—which is somehow surprising whenever it happens, even though it's the goal.

Evidence of God's presence shakes things up. When you know God's Spirit is right there, nearly tangible, you can't help but be in awe. The world shifts, in a way. You become immediately humble while also oddly confident. You hardly realize all this, of course, because all you can think about is the beauty and power of the Father.

Don't miss out on this experience. Join a prayer group, or start one. The one requirement for leading a prayer group is a heart for God.

Ask for help.

No one who achieves success
does so without acknowledging
the help of others. The wise
and confident acknowledge this
help with gratitude.

—Source Unknown

HELP

You have not because you ask not. You'd be amazed at the generosity of people if you are open to receiving from them. Write on your Facebook wall that you need something—a fan to dry up a flooded basement, a certain book for your continuing educational plans, a discount coupon to help cover your grocery bill—and you'll have many offers. Call a friend and tell her you are overwhelmed by your kids and just need an hour away from them, and she'll likely drop everything to come help you. Tell your Bible study group that you just don't know how to handle whatever crisis you are facing, and they'll load you up with meals, housecleaning, and babysitting.

It's not that everyone is sitting around bored and wealthy, wondering what they can do or give away. It's that they care about you. Your openness to them is a gift, and they honor your vulnerability with a sacrifice of their own. We may admire people who seem to have it altogether and never need anything from anyone; but the people we *love* are those who share their lives with us—warts and all.

Furthermore, by asking for help you are giving others an opportunity. They don't only get to deepen their relationship with you; they get to feel useful and valuable. It gives them a spiritual and emotional boost.

Asking for help cannot become a lifestyle of dependency; but when in genuine need, it creates a culture of interdependence.

Make yourself feel pretty.

Charm is deceptive, and beauty is fleeting; but a woman who fears the LORD is to be praised.

—Proverbs 31:30

BEAUTY

When you feel the most unhappy and would like to drown your sorrows in a bowl of ice cream, when you feel like letting your hair remain snarly, and when sweatpants and a grubby T-shirt are all you want to wear—that's the exact moment you need to get dressed up. Take a shower (maybe after you go for a run), do your hair, wear your classiest outfit, and hold your chin up. Making yourself pretty is much healthier than making yourself miserable.

Looking *put together* when you're not feeling put together is *not* to fool others; it's to help *you*. It will feel fake only when you're forcing yourself to begin, and only because the negative emotion is beginning to consume you; quickly, though, the positive action will cause the miserable feelings to subside so joy can find its way back in.

Remember though, how you look on the outside is far less important than your inner beauty. Don't let your efforts to improve yourself physically cause you to forget your real mission: to be a godly woman, made beautiful through your righteousness, which comes to you by grace.

Hug someone.

Hugs can do great amounts of good—

especially for children.

—Princess of Wales Diana

HUGS

God must have sighed in approval when He invented hugs. It's almost like hugs have a magical power. Standing for just a moment in time and giving and accepting the love of another makes the world stand still. Whether life is stressful or lonely or devastating or exciting, a hug is sometimes the only sufficient way to express our emotion and to share that experience with another person.

If you have young children and you are exhausted and frazzled, stop. Let the laundry pile up around you as you stand for a moment with your face pressed against your husband's shoulder or your baby's sweet head. It will be good for both of you.

If you are lonely and feel like you have no one to hug, think again. Go to church and replace the handshake of greeting with a hug. Call a friend or relative you haven't seen in ages and make a dinner date, soon. Reach out!

If the person you most want to hug is alienated from you due to stress in the relationship, pray. Ask God for the opportunity to hug again—even if that means you need to change or apologize or forgive.

Hug someone. It'll be a blessing to them and to you.

Don't overreact.

Anger is a momentary madness,

so control your passion or it

will control you.

—Horace

PASSION

Passion, like anything, is neutral. How it is used is what determines whether it is harmful or helpful. You can certainly use passion to inspire yourself to take action to defend the weak or to bring about social justice or to lavish love on another person. However, passion can also lead you to overreact to situations. It's wise to wait until your passion declines before you take action.

Every time you have a strong negative reaction to something, try to step back from the situation to assess what is causing that emotion. Pray for discernment. More times than not, our passion is aroused when we are personally insulted, making us highly biased. Giving in to these feelings will likely lead to an error in judgment and perhaps a regrettable action. Even if you can avoid acting out, dwelling in this emotion certainly isn't pleasant or beneficial.

Personal insults cannot simply be ignored, but they can be forgiven. Remind yourself of how Christ forgave your sins so that you can feel empowered to forgive others.

Take a nap.

For six days, work is to be done,

but the seventh day is a Sabbath

of rest, holy to the LORD.

—Exodus 31:15

REST

The secret to enjoying a good nap is to work hard beforehand. Make a to-do list, and accomplish as many items as possible; throw yourself into your work or chores or responsibilities. And when it's time to quit, quit. Set your work aside and rest.

Remember, though, rest is not recreation. Taking the family to the beach or spending the day at an amusement park or inviting friends over for a cookout is not rest. Just because you're not working, it doesn't mean you're resting. Just because you enjoy what you're doing, it doesn't mean you're resting. Leisure activities are good and healthy, but not a replacement for rest.

As a culture, we work hard and we play hard, but we don't rest easy. If we manage to sneak a nap in, we hope we don't get caught. We collapse into bed after a long day of work or play, and wake up ready to do it all over again.

God gave us a full day of rest because He knew we needed it. He also knew we'd resist it—that's why He had to make it a command. He's like the mother of a two-year-old who won't go to bed; sometimes He forces us to nap.

Give in. Rest. It's good for you.

Life isn't fair, so don't expect it to be.

Baseball is a lot like life.

The line drives are caught,

the squibbles go for base hits.

It's an unfair game.

—Rod Kanehl

BROKENNESS

In a perfect world, everyone would be kind and generous, natural disasters would be unheard of . . . and pizza would be free. In our broken world, sin has affected everything; the beautiful, perfect paradise that God had created is tainted. Life, as we know it, is not fair. No matter what we do, no matter how hard we work, no matter how good we are, life will never be fair . . . and there will be no such thing as a free lunch. Paradise will not return until Jesus does.

I do not mean to paint a gloomy picture. And you know the brokenness of this world all too well. So why am I telling you? To free you.

When we accept that life isn't fair, we lose our sense of entitlement. When we quit thinking that maybe this time things will go our way, we remove ourselves from the false belief that the world revolves around us. And when we are free from our self-centeredness, we see God more clearly.

Don't expect life to be fair. Instead, be ready to forgive when people fail you, to help when disaster strikes, and to love unconditionally.

Pay your tithe.

It is possible to give without loving,

but it is impossible to love

without giving.

—Richard Braunstein

GIVING

Giving living is the generosity test for all believers. "'Test me in this,' says the LORD Almighty, 'and see if I will not throw open the floodgates of heaven and pour out so much blessing that you will not have room enough for it'" (Malachi 3:10). Money represents so much—security, privilege, power, luxury—that it feels impossible to think that giving it away actually benefits us. Such logic defies natural laws. And yet God promises to give us more than we can ask or imagine if only we trust Him.

Matter of fact that's what tithing is: trusting God. Giving Him a tithe of our money is our way of saying we know He will provide. Tithing is not giving leftover money at the end of the month to a friend in need; tithing is not sacrificing your nest egg to buy the church something you think they need; tithing is not paying for your kids' Christian education. Tithing is consistently taking ten percent of your income and giving it to the church to use as the leadership directs. In other words, *out of obedience and trust*, you give up the money before you're sure you can pay your other bills (you might even give extra on those weeks you're especially concerned about your finances) and you give up control on how it is spent.

Giving your tithe may require that you make sacrifices—either by cutting spending or increasing income; but, in faith, you wait to see how God rewards you. It may not be what you expect. It may be much better.

Life's a river.

The only real security in a
relationship lies neither in looking
back in nostalgia, nor forward
in dread or anticipation, but living
in the present relationship and
accepting it as it is now.

—Anne Morrow Lindbergh

MOVING FORWARD

I s there a time in your life that you think fondly about? Was high school your prime time, when you were popular or athletic or at the top of your class academically? Or was your prime time when you first met the Lord and were on fire for Him? Or was your prime time everything before a tragedy struck your family?

No matter when or why it was your prime time, it's time to let that go. Make *now* your prime time. Quit looking back and start living now. That's the joy of sins forgiven.

Life is like a river. The current will start pulling you downstream toward new adventures. You can learn from where you've been. Start planning now for how you're going to handle what's coming next. Look at the scenery, survey the waterfalls, enjoy the rush of white water, rest in the lazy water. Live now as well as in the days ahead in the power of Christ.

Don't hold a grudge and you don't dwell on past mistakes; and don't over-exalt your successes. Once you understand that life is like a river, you ask Christ to get in the boat and take complete control of your life.

Quit standing on the shore and get back into life. Life's a river. Enjoy it!

Accept mystery.

And we know that in all things
God works for the good of those
who love him, who have been
called according to his purpose.

—Romans 8:28

UNDERSTANDING

Everything happens for a reason . . . but you might not ever know the reason. Once in awhile God gives us a glimpse of His divine purpose, but we never get the full picture. We can't possibly comprehend the intricacies of our interwoven lives and how one thing affects the other.

It's like we're an instrument in an orchestra, and all we hear is the bell that we strike or the violin that we play, which may sound odd or off-key by itself; but God is the conductor and He knows how all the parts play together, and He makes something beautiful out of the chaos. Or we're like the single dot on a pixilated image; we make no sense out of context, but combined with the other dots by the artist's hand, something beautiful is created.

Events in our lives may seem meaningless, and we may never fully understand why God allowed them to happen. The answer is to leave things in His hands. He promises to make all things good for those who love Him and are called according to His purpose, so we simply to need love Him. By accepting mystery we are declaring our trust in God, who has all things under control.

Turn off the radio.

The holiest of all holidays
are those kept by ourselves in
silence and apart; The secret
anniversaries of the heart.

—Henry Wadsworth Longfellow

SILENCE

Imagine dining at a restaurant that has no background music. Imagine driving in the car without having the radio on. Imagine being home without the TV running. Imagine silence. Imagine silence for hours at a time.

Does that sound good, or terrifying?

We're used to surrounding ourselves with noise. Often the sounds of life are good. Music, conversation, even entertainment are pleasant things that enhance our lives. However, when we use noise to block out the whispering of the Holy Spirit or to avoid dealing with personal wounds or to ignore the hard work of self-examination then noise becomes a problem.

If you never make time for silence, you stagnate yourself; you miss out on one of the most important and effective ways to grow. Have the courage to turn the radio off from time to time. Remove all distractions. Silence unwraps the most precious gift God has given you: yourself.

Apologize for the right things.

It takes a great deal of character strength to apologize quickly out of one's heart rather than out of pity. A person must possess himself and have a deep sense of security in fundamental principles and values in order to genuinely apologize.

—Stephen Covey

APOLOGIES

For some people, saying those two little words, "I'm sorry," is worse than getting a root canal. Other people spit them out as often as they sneeze. Why is apologizing so much harder for some than others? Why can't all of us just bite the bullet?

Maybe that is the wrong question. Perhaps we should be asking why we don't all recognize the significance of those words. Should we ask if the serial apologizer is even being sincere?

What does sorry mean? It shows regret. It means, "I wish I hadn't done that and I'll never do it again." It promises to try to make things right again. "I'm sorry" is a statement with heavy meaning and should not be spoken lightly.

Sometimes people assign different meanings to their apology. They may simply mean, "I don't want to talk about it anymore." Or, "Tell me I'm okay." Or even, "I'm not sorry at all, but I don't want you to be offended." They may not feel sorry at all for what they did.

Humbling ourselves so that we recognize we've done wrong and are willing to make amends marks us as people of integrity. Saying we're sorry when we're not says quite the opposite.

Build something.

Make it your ambition to lead a quiet
life, to mind your own business and
to work with your hands.

— 1 Thessalonians 4:11

PHYSICAL LABOR

Touch a button, and your food gets hot. Pull a switch, and your dishes get clean. Turn a knob, and your clothes get washed. We have vacuum cleaners and ride-on lawnmowers and gas fireplaces. We have motor vehicles and grocery stores.

We don't have to do much work these days. And for the labor that is required, we often hire housekeepers and lawn maintenance crews to do it.

It wasn't long ago that such a luxurious life wasn't even imagined. People worked to survive; hard physical labor was the norm for men and women in all stations of life. The disadvantages to that life were significant: people died younger, had little leisure time, and didn't travel much. This is not a lifestyle to which we would willingly go back. However, have all our improvements cost us something?

To answer this question for yourself, go do some physical labor. Build a bookshelf. Cut down an old tree. Plant and tend a garden. Clean all your windows. Paint a room. Find something productive to do with your hands, and see how it feels. You'll likely be exhausted afterwards; but you'll have a deep sense of satisfaction as well, in a way that will be new and exciting to you. Try it!

Everything is negotiable.

Honesty has a beautiful and
refreshing simplicity about it.
No ulterior motives. No hidden
meanings. An absence of hypocrisy,
duplicity, political games, and verbal
superficiality. As honesty and real
integrity characterize our lives, there
will be no need to manipulate others.

—Charles Swindoll

ACQUIESCENCE

Learning to accept "No" for an answer is something every mother tries to instill in her children. Kids will beg until they finally get their way, unless parents quickly shut down the whining and consistently stand firm in their resolve.

Some adults haven't grown out of the demanding stage. They force their own way, or whine or manipulate or sulk. They understand that everything is negotiable; it's only a matter of figuring out how to get the other person to agree. And some people are better than others at figuring it out.

It may be true that everything is negotiable, however sometimes the cost is too much. Getting your way isn't always winning.

You could convince your boss and team to accept your idea, but if you haven't given the others an opportunity to look critically at the fully-exposed idea, it could fail. You could convince your husband to buy a new living room set; but if he really didn't want that, he may end up resenting you. You may convince your church to fire the pastor; but the church may fall apart too.

Rather than getting your own way, focus on God's way. He knows better than anyone that nothing is impossible. Trust Him and He will guide you.

Read a book you normally wouldn't.

The more one reads

the more one sees

we have to read.

—John Adams

READING

You may be the type of person who loves to lose yourself in a page-turning paperback novel for hours at a time. Or you may like a good self-help book in doses. Or perhaps you're the academic type and often stick your nose in a good, hardcover nonfiction to stimulate the brain.

Whatever your preference, try something new. If you're not reading anything deep, you'll become shallow yourself. If you don't ever lighten up, you'll be out of touch. You might even need to read a book by a historian just to sharpen the brain. Read something that doesn't deal with your vocation in life. Push yourself to go beyond what is normal for you so you won't be stuck in the same old thinking pattern.

Determine to experience something new. Remember, our emotional, intellectual, physical, and spiritual sides are all interconnected, and if we get in a slump in one area, all areas are affected. If you want to grow in your faith, stretch your mind also.

Pay attention to your tone of voice.

We are not won by arguments that
we can analyze, but by tone and
temper; by the manner, which
is the man himself.

—Samuel Butler

TONE OF VOICE

People sometimes say completely inappropriate things, and then wave it off by saying, "Oh, you know what I mean." Be careful of such statements. People don't know what you're thinking, and your words and nonverbal language are all they have to go on.

That's why it's so important to be aware of what we're unintentionally communicating. For instance, it's difficult to discern the degree of our own intensity. What we express on the outside may not accurately reflect what is going on internally. If you're an outgoing type-A personality, you may not realize how zealous you come off about something you actually don't really care about, and hadn't thought about until the topic came up. If you're an intensely shy person you may think that by nodding your head you are boldly taking a stand, and end up frustrated and confused later when nobody remembers.

Often our tone of voice betrays us. You may be focused when your husband interrupts you and your response sounds short, though you don't feel angry. You may instruct your kids and they think you're yelling at them, though you're only being preventative.

Part of loving others is to make adjustments to benefit them. One way to do that is to pay attention to the tone of your voice.

No white lies.

Every violation of truth is not
only a sort of suicide in the liar,
but is a stab at the health
of human society.

—Ralph Waldo Emerson

LYING

It seems harmless to cover up some minor fault with a little white lie. You tell your husband, "The mail hasn't come yet," when you really forgot to check. You tell your boss, "I got stuck in traffic," when you were running late. You tell your kids, "They didn't have cotton candy ice cream," when you just didn't want to buy it. Nobody will ever know the truth and you don't have to be the bad person. In fact, such lies may seem to strengthen the relationship because they allow you to avoid a fight.

Lying, however, on a large or small scale, has many negative effects. The worst, is that lying reshapes your character. You may start with one little white lie, notice how easy it was, and continue to drop other lies; in time you become immune to feeling guilt, and the lies grow.

Lying also causes you to hide your weaknesses rather than face them. By confessing your shortcomings you give God an opportunity to work through the situation in a redemptive manner.

And, of course, lying erodes trust. It takes just one moment to destroy trust and many years to build it back up.

Tell the truth. It'll be better in the long run.

Make a temporary friend.

Do not forget to entertain strangers, for by so doing some people have entertained angels without knowing it.

—Hebrews 13:2

PEOPLE

We are constantly surrounded by strangers. Not only do we pass them on the streets and at shopping centers and in the hallways of our work; we talk to them. We do business with them. We sit next to them and eat next to them. And yet we hardly know they exist.

Jesus told us to love our neighbors. He told a story to illustrate what that looks like: seeing and caring for someone who is in our path. In fact, he said, "treat people the way you want to be treated."

Next time someone waits on you at a restaurant, look into her eyes and have an interest in who she is. Next time you're on the phone with a sales person, remember that he is a real person with stresses and responsibilities like you have. Next time you're at the park, strike up a conversation with another person—whether a young mom, an old homeless woman, or an elderly couple.

You don't need to exchange phone numbers or become Facebook friends, but give every attempt to at least be temporary friends with the people who cross your path. Engage them, learn from them, and bless them. Love them.

Don't worry.

Seek first his kingdom and his
righteousness, and all these things will
be given to you as well. Therefore
do not worry about tomorrow,
for tomorrow will worry about itself.
Each day has enough trouble
of its own.

—Matthew 6:33-34

WORRY

Tragedy strikes wherever we are, whatever we are doing. People have died at a local baseball field after getting hit by a ball in the bleachers. People have died in their beds when an airplane crashed directly into their house. It happens.

Other times lives are spared from impossible situations: someone shoots himself in the temple with a nail gun and lives. Someone goes over Niagara Falls and lives. It happens.

We can't control the circumstances of life. We can't control the small stuff. It may or may not rain for your picnic. Your paycheck may or may not arrive by tomorrow. Your car may or may not break down on the road.

So don't worry. Give every effort to be safe, prepare for extenuating circumstances, be wise about your plans for the future; but don't worry. Think about it: how many of the things you've worried about have actually happened? Did it turn out you were worrying for nothing? Or maybe your worst fear did take place, but was it as bad as you thought?

Live right and everything will work itself out. Trust God and He will supply your needs.

You have value.

But God demonstrates his own love
for us in this: While we were still
sinners, Christ died for us.

—Romans 5:8

WORTH

It hardly makes sense to say everybody's special. If we're all special, doesn't being extraordinary become ordinary? And yet it's true. We each have extraordinary value and dignity. You are precious to God; He loves you as if you are the only person on earth. And you are precious to others. There are billions of people in the world, but if you were to die, your loved ones would be devastated.

You are important. God has chosen you to be a part of your specific family and community. He has a plan for you, a purpose for you. Your moment of coming to salvation caused the angels in heaven to throw a giant party; your daily obedience and prayers are like beautiful incense filling God's throne room with a heavenly scent.

Next time you look in the mirror and criticize yourself, stop. Remind yourself how beautiful you are to God. Next time you mess up and think you'll never get things right, stop. Remind yourself that God has chosen you for His purpose. Next time you feel worthless, stop. Don't believe the lie. You are powerful.

You are a daughter of the King!

Stick with a budget.

If you know how to spend less
than you get, you have the
philosopher's stone.

—Benjamin Franklin

BUDGET

Ads bombard us from the radio, television, magazines, billboards, and many other places. We're told directly and indirectly that the key to our happiness is one material thing or another, and that we deserve to have good things. It's an easy message to buy. We like the idea of deserving things and then getting what we deserve, even if they don't fit in our budget.

God has riches beyond what we can imagine and He loves blessing His people with good things. Keep in mind, though, that the good things that God has for us are not always the things we think we need. Also, God doesn't use false advertising. He doesn't tell us we deserve anything—well, except death (Ro. 6:23). With God, all the good things we receive are by grace; they are undeserved gifts.

When we pursue material things rather than seeking what God wants for us, we lose the better thing. To keep yourself restrained from falling prey to materialism, create a budget—determining before you get that paycheck in your hand what you want to spend your money on—and then stick with it. God's riches are abundant and good. Honor Him by trusting Him to provide good things for you.

Don't get upset if you get blamed for something you didn't do.

When you are younger you get blamed

for crimes you never committed and

when you're older you begin to get

credit for virtues you never possessed.

It evens itself out.

—I. F. Stone

BLAME

Have you ever been falsely accused? It's a lousy feeling. Miserable, actually. I would put it up there in one of the most stress-inducing situations. The more you protest, the more guilty you look; but if you say nothing, who's going to defend you?

The obvious answer to that question is God; but let's think about how that plays out.

God knows that you are innocent of this crime, right? He knows you are being falsely accused. He's all about justice, and He has all the power. So you should be completely vindicated, right?

Of course, God also knows all the things you have done that no one else knows. He knows what you have been guilty of and things that you've never been caught doing. With that in mind, you realize His justice and power may not work to your advantage anymore.

God is gracious. When King David repented to God for some pretty horrendous sins, God accepted his cries, and called him blameless! David was made righteous and called a man after God's own heart.

God knows your heart. He knows if you are blameless. The best thing you can do when falsely accused is to sit back and let God handle the situation. Be humble. If God is okay with others thinking you did this, that's what is best. No matter what, repent of your sins and accept His grace, in whatever form it comes.

Imagine life from another person's perspective.

Winners have the ability to step back from the canvas of their lives like an artist gaining perspective. They make their lives a work of art—an individual masterpiece.

—Denis Waitley

PERSPECTIVE

Have you ever gone back to your hometown or old high school—and been shocked to discover how small everything is. You remember it larger than life. And no wonder! At the time you were living in that location, you were consumed by all that went on there. That was your world.

We can do the same thing in the life we're living right now. We don't see beyond our own little world—whether that is our household, our church, our neighborhood, our work, our children's school, our circle of friends, our hobbies, or our schedules.

To break out of the habit of being self-focused, try this exercise. Go back to a recent journal entry (or think back on recent conversations) and imagine how it would sound if a stranger read it (or heard it). Imagine more about that stranger: make her a different race, a different economic status, a different life-stage, a different political view, a different personality, from a different community. How would you sound to others? What do you need to change so that you are being compassionate, understanding, wise, and godly *from their perspective*?

Don't change for the sake of change or simply to please others. You can't please everyone, and attempting to do so would send you spinning. But do see yourself clearly and ask God to help you to change what needs to be changed.

Give the kids chores.

It is not what we get. But who we become, what we contribute . . . that gives meaning to our lives.

—Anthony Robbins

CHORES

If you let a toddler wash a mirror with you, he will leave streaks. If you ask a child to take out the trash, she'll likely forget to gather it from one room or another. If you ask a teenager to mow the grass, he'll probably rush through it and miss spots. It's much easier just to do what needs to be done yourself.

In the long run, assigning chores to your kids will help you. You'll have to be patient as you teach them how to do the work right, but if you are consistent and instructive, it will pay off.

Coaching your kids to do chores so that you can sit back and eat *bonbons* while they slave away for you is not the purpose of assigning them chores, of course. Teaching a child to work is a gift for them, and only a bonus for you. When children learn at a young age to contribute to the household, they won't take things for granted—and will likely transfer their thankfulness also to God.

Knowing how to do a job well and to stick with it until completed will also empower them to be productive adults. They will be less likely to have a sense of entitlement—as if everything should be handed to them on a silver platter—and more likely to be contributors. Not only will this help them to earn a living, it will give them a sense of purpose and a longing to serve in God's kingdom.

Don't compliment
unless it's true.

Flattery corrupts both the

receiver and the giver.

—Edmund Burke

AFFIRMATION

What should a mother do when her little boy scribbles out a picture in three seconds and boldly holds it up for praise? Of course she can't blurt out that it's horrible with absolutely no artistry to it; but should she gush about its brilliance? No. Such empty compliments eventually cause the kids to overlook her encouragement. Also, it teaches them to be satisfied with shoddy work rather than aspiring towards excellence. The best strategy in such a situation would be for the mother to say something like, "I love that you want to learn to color. Here, let me help you."

Any encouragement you give has to be based on truth. Don't tell your boss you like his new haircut if you hate it. That's flattery and does not benefit anyone. It makes you look ridiculous to your colleagues, it may cause your boss to question your judgment if he himself hates the haircut too, and it makes you feel small.

The good news is that you can almost always find something positive to say about someone if you try. It takes a few more seconds of effort, but your words will be valued and a blessing to others.

Change the furniture around.

Being stuck is a position few of us like. We want something new but cannot let go of the old—old ideas, beliefs, habits, even thoughts. We are out of contact with our own genius. Sometimes we know we are stuck; sometimes we don't. In both cases we have to DO something.

—Inga Teekens

CHANGE

Do you ever feel stuck? Do you ever feel like your life is like a train car coasting down the tracks laid out for you—and the landscape is boring? You can't go back and you can't even stop, and you can't even hope anymore for a fork in the road. Maybe you're in a job you never wanted or that turned out much different than you expected. Maybe you've lived the whole marriage, kids, empty nest pattern just because that was what was expected of you. Maybe your marriage is empty.

You need an adventure. If you keep on this path, the boredom will cause you to snap and you'll do something you'll regret.

You might not be able to change your job and you certainly can't change your husband or kids (you've probably tried), so it's time to change your environment. Change the furniture around, paint a room, hang up photographs, make new curtains, throw out junky stuff, or organize your cupboards. You don't need to move to a new place (in fact, that's running away from your problems) or spend a lot of money (that's self-medicating with consumerism). Simply take ownership of your life and make it prettier or more interesting or more functional. Learn to enjoy where you are. Let your home improvement project symbolize your life improvement.

You are not stuck on any tracks. You are right where God wants you to be. Now find out what He wants you to do there.

Drive slower.

Hasten slowly.

—Caesar Augustus

CALM

We always have so much to do and so little time to do it. The astounding improvements in technology have made life easier in some ways, but also demand we do things quicker. Since we can do everything instantly, we are expected to—whether that means getting a project to our boss or sending pictures of our family vacation to our mother. Kids want food to be ready on demand, and we often comply. We jump on fast-moving expressways to get to wherever we're going faster. Friends send text messages when we take too long (i.e., more than five minutes) to answer an email.

We need to slow down. God didn't build us to be constantly on the move; adrenaline rushes are supposed to empower us for brief intervals occasionally, not for our constant state. Our frenetic pace is going to seriously damage our physical health, if it hasn't already—not to mention our mental health.

Slowing down has to be an intentional effort. Begin in the car. Take the back roads so you'll be forced to drive slower. Follow the speed limit, or even go below it. Use cruise control if you have to so that you don't automatically start rushing the second you stop thinking about it. Enjoy the calm feeling it evokes, and let these quiet moments set the pace for the rest of your day.

Don't break the law.

The fear of the LORD

is the beginning of wisdom; all who

follow his precepts have good

understanding.

—Psalm 111:10

CITIZENSHIP

You're a law-abiding citizen, right? You don't rob banks or steal from shopping malls. You don't vandalize buildings or assault people. You probably don't even litter.

But do you speed? Do you jaywalk? Do you watch pirated movies? Do you take items from your workplace that don't belong to you? Do you pretend you don't know your sixteen-year-old needs a permit so you could take him fishing with you?

Don't break the law, even for little things. At the minimum, it's arrogant to believe that you know best; at the worst, it's disobeying God.

If you think the law is good for others, but just doesn't apply to you, think again. Anytime people put themselves above the law, they put themselves above other people. Scripture makes it clear that all are equal, and each of us will be held accountable to God.

If you think the law is wrong, don't disobey it—change it. We are blessed to live in a country where individuals are powerful, and where we have the resources to bring about changes.

Honor your parents.

Honor your father and your mother, so
that you may live long in the land the
LORD your God is giving you.

—Exodus 20:12

PARENTS

If your parents are still alive, do you talk to them every day; do you set a weekly date to touch base; do you connect only on Mother's Day and Christmas? No matter how often you talk to your parents, be sure your intentions are good. Try to go a whole conversation without asking for something, without being bitter, without criticizing them (even in your mind). Simply honor them and enjoy them.

It's easy to never break out of the habit of receiving from your parents. When you were a child, this was natural and right for them to provide for you; but the tables are turning. Show them how well they have raised you by seeking out ways to care for them. If they have hurt you in the past, ask God to help you to forgive them, even if they haven't asked for forgiveness. Quit worrying about their idiosyncrasies that drive you crazy, and get to know them as real people, not just parents. Find out what they are interested in, what they need, what matters to them. Honor them and enjoy them.

If your parents have already passed away, you are still called to honor them. Speak highly of them to others; forgive them for any real or perceived offenses; live in a way that brings honor to your family name; remember them with love.

Ask for advice and listen to it.

They that will not be counseled,
cannot be helped. If you do not
hear reason she will rap you
on the knuckles.

—Benjamin Franklin

ADVICE

It seems like everybody hates unsolicited advice; honestly, most people hate all advice. The reason it comes to us unsolicited is because we never ask for it—and people can see that we need it.

Some of us strong-willed types might ask for advice, but really we're just looking for affirmation or sympathy; we don't actually expect to make any changes. Others of us may ask for advice, but what we really want is to be told what to do; we don't want the responsibility of making a decision alone.

Advice is information from another person with a different perspective that helps you to decide what to do. In other words, the decision is still up to you, but you seriously consider what the other person has offered.

Advice is invaluable, especially from godly, wise people who love you. And unlike most precious commodities, it is almost always accessible to you if you're willing to look. Seek it out! Don't waste this wonderful gift by ignoring it or not applying it to your own knowledge, even if it came to you unsolicited. Look beyond your own perspective by welcoming the perspective of others. You will enrich your own life while blessing others.

Make a decision before you feel comfortable with it.

You will make all kinds of mistakes; but as long as you are generous and true, and also fierce, you cannot hurt the world or even seriously distress her. She was made to be wooed and won by youth. She has lived and thrived only by repeated subjugations.

—Sir Winston Churchill

ACTION

Are you the kind of person who wants to be sure everything is neat and tidy before you launch into doing it? Praying for wisdom and thinking your decisions through before acting is certainly a good thing to do, but there comes a time when you may over-think. If you have thought through every issue, asked for advice, prayed, and feel like you're getting the green light—then now it's time to take action. Nike might be on to something: *Just do it!*

Nothing will ever be certain. If you and your husband are waiting until you both feel perfectly ready to have children, the day will never come. If you're waiting until you have enough money to retire, you'll be working until they kick you out. If you don't go back to school to continue your education until your kids' braces are paid for, another expense will come up to prevent you.

It's okay to feel a bit out of control and uncertain. It makes you depend on God more. You may not know *for sure* that taking the next step is exactly what God has in mind for you, but if there are no signs indicating that it isn't, go for it. Just remain open to His leading and ready to adjust your plans.

Answer your kids' questions.

Few parents nowadays pay any regard

to what their children say

to them. The old-fashioned respect for

the young is fast dying out.

—Oscar Wilde

CHILDREN

Kids ask the strangest things that seem to come out of nowhere. Often they seem inane, pointless—and honestly rather annoying. "Why is that ant crawling over there?" "Why does the clock tick?" "Why is grass green?" "Why don't we have three eyes?" Older kids ask questions too. "What's so bad about alcohol? Why don't you like [insert political figure]? What's the point of going to church?"

Most of the questions kids ask are fairly difficult to answer. It's tempting to reply, "That's just the way it is." Resist the urge. Find out the answer to their questions even if you have to research the answer. You'll learn something new in the process; but more importantly, you'll earn trust from your kids so they will also go to you for the important questions. Also, your kids will know they are valued and important to you.

Keep in mind that as you answer their questions, they may get bored of the answer. Depending on their age and intellectual capabilities, they may want a simple answer to give them the gist of the idea. Don't go on too long, making sure they know every detail, or they'll quit asking. If they're older and the answer you give them opens the door to a whole bunch of other questions, invite them to explore the answers with you, or give them the resources to pursue the answers themselves.

Learn from your mistakes.

Never walk away from failure.

On the contrary, study it carefully and

imaginatively for its hidden assets.

—Michael Korda

MISTAKES

Dwelling in the past doesn't help anyone; but learning from our mistakes is essential for personal growth. Like a wise old fish that can take the bait off a hook without getting caught, we have to know how to live life to the fullest without getting caught in the snares of life.

Let's face it, everyone makes mistakes. But some of us make the same mistakes again, and again. Learning from mistakes and applying the principles learned so that we don't repeat the offense transforms us into wise old fish.

To learn from your mistakes, take some time to recognize what went wrong. How did you get in the mess in the first place? What should you have done differently? Also think about what resulted from the mistake, naming all the negative consequences, so that you will have an emotional aversion to repeating the error.

If you mess up at home or work, apologize. Assure the people affected by your mistake that you will not repeat it (and then don't). And be confident that this mistake has made you into a better person.

Everyone has hidden struggles.

Things are not always what they seem;

the first appearance deceives many;

the intelligence of a few perceives

what has been carefully hidden.

—Phaedrus

STRUGGLES

I t's easy to think the people you watch from afar have perfect lives, or at least much more trouble-free than your own. They have enough money to take the vacation you can only dream about; or they have a very loving marriage; or their kids are all smart and athletic; or they have meaningful and productive work; or they're friendly and afraid of nothing.

Everyone has hidden struggles—many burdens that are difficult to bear. We can't always see the full picture of people's lives, even when we know them well. They could probably quickly fill you in on all that is wrong with it, exposing their weaknesses, their pain, and their imperfections. After hearing their stories, you might end up preferring your own life. You may not have everything you want, you undoubtedly have experienced pain or loss, you may live with great regret or frustration; but to those on the outside, your life looks pretty good. It doesn't look as bad to them as it does to you.

Still, in the grand scheme of things, your original assessment was probably right. All those people who look like they have it all *kind of do*. The truth is most of us in the West *do* have pretty good lives. Even you.

Rather than focusing on what's not so great about your life, celebrate what you do have.

Impress the right people.

Be more concerned with your character than with your reputation. Your character is what you really are while your reputation is merely what others think you are.

—Dale Carnegie

FAVOR

We like to say that we don't care what people think of us, but if we're completely honest, we do care. Most of us care very much, even to the point of adjusting our behavior to gain the approval of others.

Caring what people think of us is not always a bad thing. Adjusting our behavior to not offend, or to make someone happy, or to calm a stressful situation is often an admirable thing to do. It simply shows we love others as ourselves, which is exactly what Jesus taught us to do.

For sure, we can't please everyone. If we try, we will feel compelled to do opposing things simultaneously: keep quiet and speak boldly, work more hours and be home more often, go out with the girls and snuggle at home with the kids. So what do you do?

You don't have to be told to consider your own needs and desires; that comes naturally. But a hint that may help is this: know who to impress. Jesus concerned Himself with the poor and weak, and He spoke harshly to the rich and powerful. Don't worry about what the powerful think of you; worry about the weak.

Be comfortable with the poor.

If I give all I possess to the poor

and surrender my body to the flames,

but have not love, I gain nothing.

—1 Corinthians 13:3

COMPASSION

When you stop at a corner and someone knocks on your window begging for money, how do you feel? If you have to drive through a poor section of town, do you pray your car doesn't break down? Have you ever volunteered in a homeless shelter but made sure you organized the pantry so you didn't actually have to deal with the people?

If you feel uncomfortable around the poor, you need to be with them more. It's not enough to send in your monthly check to sponsor an overseas child. It's not enough to drop off food in the basket at church for the annual thanksgiving food run. You have to see their faces and hear their stories. You have to know them.

When Jesus met people in need, He saw them and had compassion on them. That's different than feeling sorry for them, and it's certainly not feeling superior to them. He saw them as real people with God-given dignity—who were in need.

We can't know people the way Jesus did, especially with only a glance. But we can get to know them by spending time with them, listening to their stories, and letting go of our preconceived notions. By loving the poor we are being most like Jesus, so it is a worthwhile pursuit.

Delegate to the right person.

You can delegate authority, but you can never delegate responsibility for delegating a task to someone else. If you picked the right man, fine, but if you picked the wrong man, the responsibility is yours—not his.

—Richard E Krafve

DELEGATING

Giving an important task to another person is risky. Sometimes it seems safer and even easier to get done what needs to be done by doing it yourself. You're more confident of your quality of work, you know you'll get it done by the deadline, and you have the most passion for it.

Delegating, as you probably already know, is important for success, whether the project is for church, work, or home. The tricky part is to find the right person to delegate a job to. Choosing the right person will benefit you, the project, and even the other person.

Letting go of some of your workload frees you up to do the things that may be a higher priority. It's easy to think that everything is important, but the fact is that you don't have time to do everything that is good. You have to use your time wisely so you will not neglect your relationship with God and others.

Before assigning a task, be sure the person has an aptitude for the work. If you give the task to the first warm body you encounter, you will likely get shoddy work and the project will suffer. It takes some effort to discover what people are good at and what is important to them, but it's worth it.

Selecting someone to do the work also honors that person. She may need the affirmation, she may need the productivity, she may need the money, or she may need the connection. Trust others, not just to the point that they can live up to your expectations, but that they might even be better than you.

Respect your husband.

Don't expect to build up the weak

by pulling down the strong.

—Calvin Coolidge

MARRIAGE

Scripture tells men and women to respect each other. This means that you get the joy and pleasure of building up your man. This entry could as easily be written the other way around—telling men to honor their wives—but this is a book for women.

Tell your husband what he does well. Trust me, he's probably much more aware of his weaknesses than he lets on, and doesn't need any reminders about that. Don't try to change him or improve him. If he's not living up to his potential, you can still find some things he's doing well. Focus on that. Tell him often—daily, even several times daily—the good things you see in him. Brag about him to others so he knows you're proud to be with him. Look for ways to privately admire him; you don't even need to share it with him, but your attitude of appreciation will show through.

Your husband will certainly fail you at times and his weaknesses will be hard to ignore. When that happens, keep your thoughts to yourself. Don't complain to him, and certainly don't complain to others. Don't even complain to yourself or God. If the mistake was minor, your lack of attention to it will cause it to fade even from your own thoughts. If the mistake was significant, you can address it later, when you're not caught up in the heat of the moment. Ask God for wisdom and favor, and then at the right time address the issue as neutrally as possible, still giving him honor and respect.

Help someone else succeed.

The glory of friendship is not in the outstretched hand, nor the kindly smile, nor the joy of companionship; it is in the spiritual inspiration that comes to one when he discovers that someone else believes in him and is willing to trust him.

—Ralph Waldo Emerson

SUPPORT

It's always fun to get the big prize at an awards banquet, to have all those people congratulate you for your success. But that kind of glory fades quickly. Not only do others forget—or worse, get turned off—by your success; it doesn't carry over to eternity.

Helping someone else succeed, without any regard for your own glory, is much more satisfying. Not only is it deeply satisfying, it has eternal significance. This kind of radical and genuine love for others is what you take with you to the other side.

Anyone who has children knows to some degree what it means to wish ultimate success to others instead of yourself. You want your kids to be more successful, happier, healthier, and more beautiful than yourself; and you do everything in your power to make that happen.

Have you ever tried doing this for anyone else, though? See what it feels like to give someone at work a good idea, without ever taking credit; you could even go so far as to help your coworker succeed with your idea by helping him or her along the way. Or give away knowledge so that others may benefit from what you know too. Try volunteering at church with something as mundane as folding the bulletins or teaching the smallest Sunday school class.

Your kids are
not you.

Parents can only give good advice

or put them on the right paths,

but the final forming of a person's

character lies in their own hands.

—Anne Frank

IDENTITY

Whether your kids are extraordinarily gifted or extraordinarily good at messing up their lives—or somewhere in between—you need to be able to separate your identity from theirs. Your kids are not you; you are not your kids.

Kids figure out the identity issue around the age of two, but parents often try to keep the umbilical cord connected for much longer. We sometimes push them to succeed in areas where we failed (or succeeded) so they can live out our dreams; instead we need to encourage them to pursue their own dreams, to follow God's calling for their own lives. We sometimes feel embarrassed and culpable when they make wrong choices, attempting to cover it up so no one will know; instead we need to hold them accountable for their actions so they will have an opportunity for change, and we need to turn to others for support, wisdom, and prayer.

Teach your kids well, and raise them up to make good choices; but don't make the mistake of thinking that you can make good choices for them—especially when they are no longer living with you. Pray for them, love them, advise them, but never try to live their lives for them.

Get a manicure.

Femininity appears to be one of
those pivotal qualities that is so
important no one can define it.

—Caroline Bird

FEMININITY

I don't care whether you're the kind of woman who likes having the door held open for her, or if the very idea makes you bristle. Whether you like chivalry or demand equal rights, you are a woman—and that is a good thing.

What does it mean to you to be woman? What are the things about being female that make you proud? What are the things about being female that you wish you could change? Do you feel empowered as a woman without losing your femininity? Do you feel feminine without losing your strength?

It's exciting that so many women are earning prominent positions in the workplace, and that home duties are being shared by husbands and wives. Scripture tells us that men and women are equal—but it cannot be denied that we are different.

God created man and woman in His image, and surely He must delight in the characteristics that define us as one gender or the other. If God delights in you being a woman, so should you! Go for a girls' night out or a women's retreat to connect with your sisters in Christ. Get a manicure or get your hair styled so you can feel beautiful. Whatever makes you celebrate your womanhood, do it!

Keep your kids innocent as long as possible.

Once you bring life into the world, you must protect it.

—Elie Wiesel

PROTECTION

We are, in part, shaped by our culture—for better or worse. Sometimes we're not even aware of how the culture is influencing us, and we have to pray that God will open our eyes to see it.

Our children, even at a very young age, are also influenced by the world around them. It is the job of the parent to protect them from its negative influences, and to teach them how to respond to it appropriately.

The trick is to balance protecting them and equipping them. Our instinct may be to hide them from the world—by not allowing television, or sending them to private schools, or living in a rural area, or handpicking their friends; or we may feel compelled to teach them how to survive in the world—by letting them fight their own battles with their friends and siblings, by not bailing them out when they forget homework assignments, by making them earn their wins in board games or sports, by traveling with them to foreign places.

Whatever your instinct is, follow it; but also do the other. Keep your kids innocent as long as possible—protecting them from materialism, racism, hatred, violence, immorality, and the like—while also teaching them to handle the obstacles.

If you are going to err on one side or the other, let it be the side of innocence. You can't give a child too much love or too much security.

Laugh with your kids.

True humor springs not more from the
head than from the heart. It is
not contempt; its essence is love.
It issues not in laughter, but in still
smiles, which lie far deeper.

—Thomas Carlyle

LAUGHTER

A mother's job is not to be her children's friend—at least not primarily. A mom is to nurture, provide for, teach, discipline, and guide her children; and all those roles require her to be a leader, not a peer. Even the love a mother lavishes on her children is different than the love peers give each other. Your love for your kids is abundant and unconditional; your kids simply can't give back to you what you give to them, and you don't expect them to.

Even so—even though you are more than a friend to your kids—you still get to behave as a friend with them from time to time. You get to play with them, share life experiences with them, and best of all laugh with them. Laughing together is probably the most bonding experience you can have. You create good memories, inside jokes that can carry on for years to come, and positive feelings for each other.

It's tough to intentionally create genuinely funny moments, but you can't just wait for them to happen spontaneously either. You have to be open to humor by managing your mood. If you keep yourself positive and pleasant most of the time—even when things aren't going your way—laughter will come easier to you, plus others around you will be open to cracking jokes.

Don't try to be funny. Just be happy. The laughter will follow.

Do a Bible study with your kids.

With flattery he will corrupt those who
have violated the covenant,
but the people who know their
God will firmly resist him.

—Daniel 11:32

BIBLE STUDY

It's exciting when your kids declare love for God and when they make a commitment to Christ. It's what every Christian parent is praying for and longing for.

Be careful, though, not to let them get carried away on emotion alone. Celebrate the joy of their decision, certainly—even extravagantly; but also make sure they are committing themselves to the one true God and not some figment of their imagination. A lot of people say they believe in God, but really know nothing about Him; they call themselves Christians but don't even know what they believe. They believe good things about Him, but not necessarily true things.

Help your children to know the Lord by studying the Scriptures with them. They won't get to know Him by listening to what the world says about Him. Give your kids the most precious gift of all—the Truth. Introduce them to Jesus by reading the living and powerful Word of God.

At the very least, read the Bible together on a regular basis—daily, if you can. Talk about what you've read and offer a prayer in response. Or be more proactive and buy an age-appropriate Bible study that you can work through together. Bible studies will help them to go deeper and to discover more about to whom they are giving their lives. It will be a beautiful experience for both of you.

Pray with your husband.

Sometimes the answer to prayer
is not that it changes life, but
that it changes you.

—James Dillet Freeman

PRAYER

Praying with another person is an intimate experience. When you seek God together, you have a shared spiritual experience that joins you in a profound way. Pray with your husband. Not only will your relationship with God blossom, the bond with your husband will be strengthened.

If your husband is not a believer, it may feel awkward to invite him to pray; but you won't know if he's willing until you ask. If you make your time of prayer focused entirely on honoring God and seeking His will (and not a time to lecture your husband in the form of a prayer), your husband may experience the presence of God for the first time—and come to anticipate your time together as much as you do.

If your husband is a godly man, but you still don't pray together, he may be pleasantly surprised by the suggestion. He may want the accountability to be faithful in this spiritual discipline as much as you do.

If inviting your husband to pray is awkward because your relationship is strained, this may be exactly what you need. Agree to make prayer a neutral time together, and see what happens.

Don't overdo it.

Moderation is an ostentatious proof of
our strength of character.

—Francois de La Rochefoucauld

MODERATION

Y ou know how you can kill a plant by watering it too much? That's sort of how life is. You can overdo it. Just as the plant needs a small amount of water on a regular basis, so it is with your life.

We tend to glorify big things, extravagant things, in this generation; but moderation is often harder, and better, than the extreme. You might be gracious and forgiving of a major wrong committed against you, for example, but hold a grudge for daily annoyances. You might start a huge exercise program, but lose interest after the first day. You might be able to fast for several days, but then you go right back to eating too much.

It's just as the old fable teaches: The perseverance of the turtle is better than the speed of the hare. Don't get distracted from the goal.

We are naturally drawn to one extreme or another; after all, bigger is better and greatness is supreme, right? Balance is not quite as exciting, and it's tricky to achieve. But balance is what keeps you stable; giving in to one extreme or another sets you up for a fall.

Rather than pursuing greatness, pursue goodness.

Don't buy what you don't want.

Now if I do what I do not want to do,
it is no longer I who do it, but it is sin
living in me that does it.

—Romans 7:20

ABSTINENCE

Have you ever gone shopping for a specific item, but couldn't find exactly what you wanted? What did you do? Did you buy something that would be good enough, or did you wait until you were able to find exactly what you needed?

Don't buy what you don't want. Whether it's a big-ticket item—like furniture or a car or a home—or if it's a little thing like a candy bar or toothpaste or a pen, there is no point in spending your money on something that is less than ideal. You will later regret the purchase that you're now stuck with. Waiting is worth the effort.

This is more than a lesson against collecting junk. Knowing what to walk away from has spiritual significance as well. When you exercise the ability to turn down material things that do not benefit you, you can translate that to your spiritual life. Don't buy what you don't want. Don't buy the lie that you are not precious to God. Don't add habits to your life that are destructive. Don't collect grudges.

Don't take into your life the things that you will regret being stuck with.

Let them grow up.

The finest inheritance you can give to a child is to allow it to make its own way, completely on its own feet.

—Isadora Duncan

LETTING GO

When the kids are little, it seems impossible that you will ever have alone time again. It's tempting to count down the days until they'll start kindergarten, or until they'll get their driver's license, or until they graduate from high school so that you can have your life back. It's not that you don't love them like crazy; it's just that the busyness of this stage of life is exhausting.

And then something mysterious happens. They grow up. And you don't want them to leave.

Whatever you're stage—whether it's beginning a family, bustling through the elementary years, or emptying the nest—enjoy where you are. But even as you're enjoying your family in the here and now, be thinking ahead about how to let them go. It's not about rushing them out of the house so you can get your life back; it's about nurturing them into independent and responsible young adults so they can begin theirs.

Don't hold them back by babying them too long; work constantly toward letting them go. Don't cling to them when they're ready; send them out with a mission to serve God in the world.

By letting them go—yes, even preparing them to go—you will gain a friend rather than lose a child.

Pray for your kids.

I remember my mother's prayers
and they have always followed me.
They have clung to me all my life.

—Abraham Lincoln

A MOTHER'S PRAYER

Mothers have a special kind of persevering love for their kids. Fathers may get exasperated and ready to give up when their kids stray, but mothers believe in their kids when believing is no longer logical.

This kind of love has power. It compels you to pray for your kids with deep and transforming faith—and your kids feel it. Not only do they gain security from your radical love, creating an environment for change; your loving and committed prayers unleash God's power so that the impossible becomes possible.

This kind of prayer springs forth spontaneously from a mother's heart; but it can also be nurtured with structured and intentional times of prayer. Listen to your children, ask them how you might pray for them; and then set aside time to lift them up to the Father. You might pray for them alone so you can cry out without concerning yourself with their interpretation; or you can pray for them in their presence so they immediately feel the blessing.

It doesn't matter if your words are elegant or not; simply let your heart speak to God on their behalf.

Work hard.

In order to excel, you must be
completely dedicated to your chosen
sport. You must also be prepared
to work hard and be willing to accept
destructive criticism. Without
100 percent dedication, you won't
be able to do this.

—Willie Mays

LABOR

What does a hard day's work look like to you? Is it determined by the number of hours you sit at your desk, or by how much housework you get done, or by how much money you make, or by how much physical labor you get, or by how tired you are by the time you plop into bed?

Whatever measure you use, don't allow yourself to cheat. Be like your own drill sergeant and expect more of yourself than you thought possible. Instead of thinking about how much you can get away with, consider how much more you can push yourself. Instead of telling your boss or coworker or husband or friend or fellow volunteer that something isn't your job, see if you can accomplish your own task plus something else in the allotted time. Take the initiative to figure out what needs to be done; determine the most productive method for achieving the result; work hard for as long as you can.

You need to make time for rest and recreation too, of course; but during your working hours—whether the task is for pay or accomplishment or duty—invest yourself fully. In this way you will feel the satisfaction of a job well done, and you'll experience in part the joy of labor as God first created it.

Read a different version of the Bible.

It is Christ Himself, not the Bible, who is the true word of God.

The Bible, read in the right spirit and with the guidance of good teachers, will bring us to Him. We must not use the Bible as a sort of encyclopedia out of which texts can be taken for use as weapons.

—C.S. Lewis

SCRIPTURE

The Bible is an easy book to fall in love with if you devote yourself to studying it and meditating on it regularly. Many Christians have devotions nearly every day, and some commit to reading the entire Bible every year.

All this time in the Word gives you familiarity with the Scriptures, especially if you memorize passages; such familiarity can be comforting and meaningful. Verses come to mind at just the right moment, proving again and again how the Word is living and active.

It can happen, however, that even the most devout Christian becomes bored, or loses interest, or finds herself in a funk. The temptation when this happens is to quit reading Scripture for awhile. That while can turn into a longer while, and soon the habit of spending time with God disappears altogether.

One way to revive your love for the Word is to freshen the experience by using a different version of the Bible. You will remember the old familiar version as you read the new translation, but the different word choices and sentence structures will help you to understand the words in a new way.

See yourself as a servant.

You know you have a servant's
attitude when you react like a servant
when you're treated like a servant.

—Lorne Sanny

SERVANTHOOD

Jesus empowered women. He recognized their ability and authority to be leaders. He accepted them as disciples and friends. Jesus did not condone a patriarchal mindset.

Keep in mind, however, that His empowerment of women meant His admonitions to men were also to women; in other words, His overriding theme of humility, of serving each other in love and submission, was equally for women as it was for men. The very fact that Christ accepts you as an important part of the work of His kingdom means that you have to consider yourself a servant. It's a strange paradox, isn't it?

Servanthood is as humble as it sounds. Though we use words like servant-leader in very positive terms, the act of submitting to another *by its very nature* lowers the servant to a spiritual status beneath the person she is serving. Servanthood is a position of humility; however, it isn't demeaning. Jesus Himself—the very Son of God—made Himself a servant to humans . . . without losing any of His divine glory.

Consider yourself a servant to others, and live accordingly.

Pursue your dreams.

We have different gifts, according to
the grace given us. If a man's gift is
prophesying, let him use it in proportion
to his faith. If it is serving, let him
serve; if it is teaching, let him teach;
if it is encouraging, let him encourage;
if it is contributing to the needs of
others, let him give generously; if it is
leadership, let him govern diligently;
if it is showing mercy,
let him do it cheerfully.

—Romans 12:6-8

DREAMS

You are outrageously good at something. You may not even know it. If someone were to ask you about yourself—maybe during icebreakers at a Bible study—you might not even mention your passion; you might not even think of it. Sometimes the things that we are especially good at come so naturally to us that we can't even fathom them as skills. It's too easy.

Maybe you have the gift of faith, easily believing the promises of God and living in that confidence; but you sort of think everyone must do that. You may have a forgiving heart and wonder why people marvel at the ease in which you move on from sticky or hurtful situations. Maybe you have excellent memory, or natural musical ability, or a knack for organizing things, or an ability to cast a vision and generate enthusiasm.

Figure out what your gifts are, and use them. You shouldn't be surprised to discover that your career dreams fit well with your spiritual gifts and that should inspire you to pursue your dreams. Be bold. Be enthusiastic. Be ready to use your gifts for the glory of God and to build up His kingdom in whatever work He places you.

Don't work for the praise of others.

Don't work for the praise of men,
work to hear Christ say well done.

—Talmadge Johnson

EXCELLENCE

When you do something well, it's nice to get kudos, isn't it? The thing is, even if you do get praised for some achievement, it can't possibly be enough. No one will fully comprehend all that it took to accomplish that task. And more likely than not, you won't get any acknowledgement at all of what you have done.

Working for the praise of others is a dead end. At best, it's a disappointment; at worst, it is as enticing and as empty as a drug.

Work instead for the Lord; let Him be your boss. Let everything you do be excellent, even if no one but you will know it. Clean that window in the room no one enters. File those papers that have been stacked under your desk for months. Make that phone call you could get away with neglecting.

Two cautions: First, don't be such a perfectionist that you get caught up in the minute details instead of the main task. Do what needs to be done well, and let the rest go. Second, don't try to earn your way to heaven. It can't be done, no matter how stellar your work. Do good work, but accept grace. Having faith is the only way to please God.

Be confident.

Conceit is bragging about yourself.
Confidence means you believe
you can get the job done.

—Johnny Unitas

CONFIDENCE

Women sometimes think that to be attractive they have to be physically fit, nicely dressed, and well-groomed. All of that helps, of course, but the most attractive feature in a person is confidence. This is a valuable lesson for anyone who wants to be appealing to others. Whether you are dating, making friends, looking for work, or strengthening existing relationships, be aware that your poise and self-possession will impact the other person's perception of you more than anything else.

Poise cannot be faked. Your confidence has to come from a place deep inside. When you understand how loved you are by the Almighty God, you will not be intimidated. Because of God's work in your life, you will know you are worthy, and beautiful, and strong, and wise. And your confidence will surround you as surely as the air you breathe.

Don't confuse confidence with bossiness. Pushing other people around is something entirely different than poise, and actually unattractive. If you are in a position of authority or in a mutual relationship, let your understanding of how loved you are by God shape the way you interact with others—since they too are loved by the Father.

Communicate right.

Science and technology multiply around us. To an increasing extent they dictate the languages in which we speak and think. Either we use those languages, or we remain mute.

—J. G. Ballard

COMMUNICATION

Some people still pick up a fountain pen and stationary to write a lovely note to a friend or loved one; but most people don't. We have telephones and email accounts and cell phones and Facebook pages to do our communications; and such technology can be used effectively to communicate in meaningful ways. But because it's easier, it doesn't mean it's inferior.

Written letters are wonderful, and can be just the right method for connecting with someone else; however, such communication has to be used as a supplement, not the main thing. Current technology simply moves too fast, and traditional letter writing can't keep you caught up on the life of your loved ones.

Understanding how to text, instant message, Facebook chat, and Skype is essential for optimal connection, especially with the younger generation or with loved ones far away. Don't let the world move on without you. You don't have to spend hours a day having shallow conversations with people you once knew; how you use the technology is up to you, and you can focus your attention on only those with whom you wish to maintain a relationship.

Get it done.

Procrastination is the thief of time.

— Charles Dickens

PROCRASTINATION

Procrastination is a terrible enemy of productivity, and yet many of us give in to it on a regular basis. Sometimes our to-do list is so long that just writing it out takes all day. When we're that overwhelmed it's hard to know where to focus our time and energy, so we end up doing nothing. Deadlines approach and we start to panic; panic only makes us less productive and we fall further behind.

I could recite the old cliché and admonish you not to put off until tomorrow what you can do today; but you probably know that one and it hasn't changed a thing for you so far. So what do you do to cure a bad case of procrastination?

Start with the little things. Or start with the big things. Start with the things you dislike the most. Or start with the things you love. It doesn't matter. Just start. Don't over think it. Don't agonize over what you feel like doing. Don't take any time at all to consider what would work best in the grand scheme of things. Just start. Now. Go.

Be who you want them to be.

We are always getting ready to
live, but never living.

—Ralph Waldo Emerson

LIVING

Do you wish your friends were sophisticated, or maybe down-to-earth? Do you wish you had more friends from other cultures to expand your horizons, or maybe a tight group of friends? Do you wish you could find a boyfriend who loves the Lord, or a boss who cares about the environment, or a pastor who reaches out to the community, or a husband who will go on a diet with you?

What you want in another person you have to first find in yourself. If you're looking for stimulating conversation, don't sit on your couch every Friday night watching re-runs on TV. If you want to hang out with people who are active, find a Saturday morning cycling group and join them. If you want a Christ-centered relationship with your husband, make Christ the center of your life.

Be the person you want to be, and you will attract like-minded people.

Don't expect instant transformation of the people you are trying to influence. In fact, don't expect any transformation at all. Focus on being the person you want to be, and let God take care of the rest.

Your weaknesses are your strengths.

Let us speak, though we show all our faults and weaknesses, — for it is a sign of strength to be weak, to know it, and out with it — not in a set way and ostentatiously, though, but incidentally and without premeditation.

—Herman Melville

WEAKNESSES

So, you're not good at something. If you're just figuring that out now, you're the last one to know. Everyone has weaknesses, and those weaknesses are definitely evident to others. Don't bother trying to cover yours up because that would simply reveal a bigger weakness—that you are not comfortable with yourself. It would be like trying to bite out the hole in the donut; you'd only make it bigger and more obvious.

Here's the good news: your weaknesses can also be your strengths. If you have terrible memory, you probably don't hold a grudge. If you are hypersensitive, you are probably quite compassionate. If you talk too loud, you're probably a great public speaker.

It goes both ways, though. Your strengths can be your weaknesses. If you are very organized, you probably lack spontaneity. If you are good at making everyone laugh, you probably are a bit of an attention-hog.

Think of this double-edged sword as a gift to you: You can never get too down on yourself or develop too big of an ego. God has built in a system for keeping yourself in check. All you have to do is keep your eyes open and recognize how your weaknesses are your strengths, and vice versa.

Get involved in church.

There's no such thing as a solitary Christian.

—John Wesley

CHURCH

Whether you grew up in the church or have rarely set foot in the place, it's where you belong. If you have accepted Christ as your Lord and Savior, you bear his name—Christian—and you immediately have the privilege of being a part of the family of God.

The church is full of people like you—folks who are far from perfect. There might even be a few hypocrites in the mix. But God performs a miracle that would startle us if we thought about it very long: He transforms us into something beautiful.

We are the Bride of Christ; we together are being prepared to come before Him dressed in pure white. We are the body; we, together, create something bigger than ourselves. We are the army of heaven; one day we will take our place in the great battle that will defeat the Enemy.

We worship together. We pray together. We serve together. We grow together.

Don't miss out on this opportunity. Put aside your old wounds, your fear of commitment, your busyness, your apathy—and get involved.

Quit wasting time.

If time be of all things the most
precious, wasting time must be
the greatest prodigality.

—Benjamin Franklin

ACTION

We're busy people—but we're also bored. We have too much to do, but we have nothing meaningful to do. We rush from one place to another, but we don't make a difference anywhere. We chat with many people, but don't really connect with anyone.

Time is running. Every moment, every second, of your life is one moment, one second, gone. You will never get it back again.

How will you account for your time in the end? If it could be laid out in a bar graph, imagine what you would see. Would you be happy with the results? What would you have spent your time on the most? Would you have played computer games more than you prayed? Would you have brushed your hair more than you talked to your husband?

What's important to you? Decide now, and let your actions show it. Fill your time not only with good things, but with meaningful things. What would God have you do? What is He calling you to? You have just one lifetime to fulfill that calling—are you using your time wisely?

About the Authors

 Stan and Linda Toler have been married for over 37 years. The Tolers have written three previous books together.

Stan Toler is a general superintendent emeritus in the Church of the Nazarene. He served for 40 years as a pastor in Ohio, Florida, Tennessee, and Oklahoma. Toler has been an international speaker and seminar leader in churches and corporations around the world.

Toler has written more than 90 books, including his best-sellers, *God Has Never Failed Me, but He's Sure Scared Me to Death a Few Times, ReThink Your Life,* and his popular Minute Motivators series.

Linda is an educator and author who speaks from the heart to women of all ages at conferences and retreats.

Visit www.StanToler.com
to contact the authors.